To

From

The Life and
Times
of the
Rose

All illustrations in this book, unless otherwise
indicated, are taken from original paintings
by the author.

THE LIFE AND TIMES OF
THE ROSE

An essay on its history
with many of the author's own paintings

FLEUR COWLES

William Morrow and Company, Inc.
New York

It is the policy of William Morrow and Company, Inc., and its imprints and affiliates,
recognizing the importance of preserving what has been written, to print the books we
publish on acid-free paper, and we exert our best efforts to that end.

Library of Congress Cataloging-in-Publication Data

Cowles, Fleur.
    The life and times of the rose : an essay on its history with many of the author's own
paintings / Fleur Cowles.
       p.   cm.
    ISBN 0-688-12082-2 : $14.50
    1. Roses—History. I. Title.
SB411.45.C68   1992
635.9'33372—dc20   92-17714
                                                CIP

Printed in the United States of America

First Edition

1 2 3 4 5 6 7 8 9 10

BOOK DESIGN BY BOOK PRODUCTION SERVICES

INTRODUCTION

This volume owes its life to a speech I made in Los Angeles at a benefit for the historic Banning House Museum. When preparing it, I realised there was more, much more, than I could condense in any one talk, so I continued by writing this book. The museum event was a success so I hope this expanded version will give knowledge and pleasure to readers as well.

Fleur Cowles
London 1991

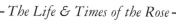

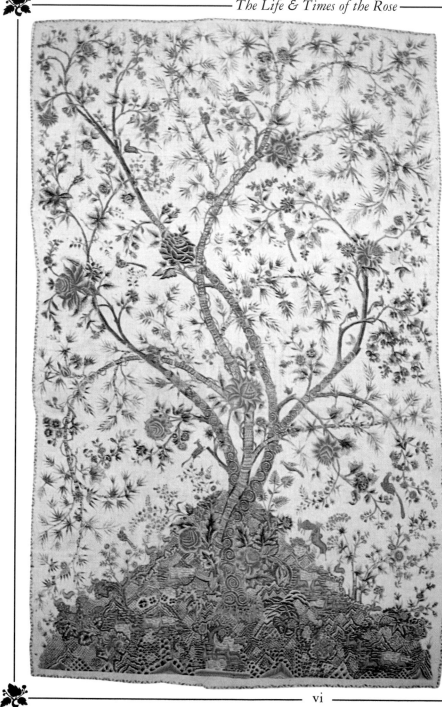

The Tree of Life. Roses have existed on earth longer than man

How long has the rose bloomed? Throughout our days it stands apart, divided from other flowers by its ancient lineage and participation in cultural history. It has inspired the beauty of Renaissance art, provided poets, writers and musicians with endless inspiration.

We know that roses have existed on earth longer than man, as is shown by fossil evidence dating back over thirty million years. One is in the collection of a Montana museum in the United States. It must have been the pale pink wild rose that we still know. Then from the Bronze Age, a mere four thousand years or so ago, another fossil of this same dog rose was found in Switzerland and fossilised rose leaves near Bonn and in Croatia. Others are in museums throughout the world, from Tonkin in China to Africa and Asia.

The Koran placed the rose in the Garden of Paradise, even before the Garden of Eden. And did you know that on 11 October 1492 Christopher Columbus recorded in his log that sailors found a bouquet of roses floating amid the flotsam of the sea to welcome them to America? Later Captain John Smith found thickets of wild roses planted by American Indians.

Rhodes 4th-century BC. The reverse of a drachma coin showing the Rhodian rose

RIGHT: *Knossos— at the top of the Grand Staircase are columns of Cretan rosettes*

The oldest *living* rose is a tree against the apse of the cathedral crypt at Hildesheim in West Germany, supposedly commemorating a tale about Kaiser Ludwig the Righteous who had been separated from his escort while hunting. He spent the night in the forest alone; but on returning home realised he'd lost a sacred relic, which was later found beneath a wild rose near his sleeping place. Legend has it that the rose 'refused' to move, so Ludwig built a chapel close to the spot, finishing it in AD 815. In 1884 the rose was treated for age, given new soil and drainage. During World War II, Allied bombs were dropped nearby and the rose caught fire but, because the root stock was undamaged the tree survived. In ancient times The Greeks used to burn their rose bushes deliberately, to encourage a good crop the following year and prevent the main stem becoming woody.

Close to the River Euphrates, in the country now known as Iraq, an ancient Sumerian born some five thousand years ago sculpted a thorn bush with a ram caught by his horns. On one leafy tip he modelled a golden rose. At Knossos in Crete archaeologists found a mural containing a pink five-petalled rose, painted some time before an earthquake shattered the palace around 1450 BC.

Excavations in Crete also uncovered rose-bedecked vessels and jewellery – pins of gold topped with a rose in full bloom and chalices decorated with sprays of blooms.

From Crete the inspiration spread to Egypt and from there to Rome where roses instantly became synonymous with debauchery, indulgence and lust. Hadn't Cleopatra proved the potent value of the rose as an aphrodisiac? Hadn't she welcomed Antony's barge standing in a carpet of roses up to her knees and then, to woo him, covered her bed with fresh roses every day in preparation?

Soon Antony's own country was intoxicated by the idea, and the Romans outdid the queen by importing shiploads of roses from Egypt; millions arrived in rose-crowded galleys. When the Latin satirist Martial saw the Emperor Domitian receive a gift of a shipful of roses,

LEFT: An Allegory with Venus and Cupid by Bronzino. Roses were used to represent many emotions in such paintings. The cherub on the right is about to shower Venus and Cupid with roses

he wrote: 'Send *us* wheat, O Egyptians, and we shall send *you* roses in return.' To keep them fresh, the Egyptians used copper basins or amphorae. The minerals that dissolved into the roses' water extended their lives for up to six days at sea.

Roman gentlemen required roses by the ton until they became a national mania, adorning the tombs of the dead and celebrating the living by crowning new babies in rose circlets. Slaves were decorated with roses to serve food to nobles – who consumed rose pudding, rose honey, crystallised rose petals, rose vinegar and then washed themselves in rose-water.

Banquets were living paintings – a bower of roses and petal-covered tables with floors carpeted in thousands. Guests dropped roses in wine, hoping by that simple act to postpone the inevitable drunkenness which followed. Nero rained down rose petals through holes in the ceiling, falling like confetti on his guests – some were suffocated. The playfulness cost an amount equal in today's money to £50,000 each time. Roman ladies made beauty packs of rose petals, hoping to smooth out wrinkles.

Romans instructed their heirs where to plant roses and stipulated that their petals were to be scattered over their monuments. Victorious armies were welcomed on rose-covered streets and statues wore fresh crowns of roses daily.

So important to the ritual of life were they that fertile fields were converted from olive groves and food production to grow roses – for there was much more money in this cash crop. Flowers were forced to bloom out of season by a network of hot water pipes in special rooms or heated by tubs filled with hot water. The greenhouse was born.

When Saladin, the Emperor of Egypt and Syria, conquered Jerusalem in 1187, he sent rose-water carried on five hundred camels to 'clean' the Oman mosque – just as Mohammed II did to the Church of St Sophia in 1458.

With the Crusades, east-to-west traffic steadily increased. Adventurous Crusaders and unnamed travellers all seemed to have a special thought for roses, bringing them home from each excursion along with bits of stone from the Holy Sepulchre, sacred nails and fragments of the True Cross.

The twelfth century was the great age of the cathedral, in part due to the rose as it slowly became infused with religious ideas. The single flower with five petals came to be defined as a religious emblem of martyrs, also representing the virginity of Mary and the five wounds of Christ. To many people the rose *is* the Virgin Mary – and an inseparable symbol of devotion.

ABOVE: *South row window in Angers Cathedral, France. Representing Christ in Majesty surrounded by the twelve signs of the Zodiac*

LEFT: *The Coronation of the Virgin by Velázquez. The rose and the Virgin have become inseparable to many*

A Madonna without a rose in her hand is a rarity. In a rare religious painting by Velázquez, the *Coronation of the Virgin* which hangs in Madrid's Prado Museum, God the Father is placing a chaplet of red and white roses over Mary's head.

The rose window set in the brow of great churches became the Gothic disc of celestial colour which we so admire. The rose is supreme in those dazzling circles of light, often monumental in size – a flower of stone set in brilliant glass.

Soon roses decorated shrines, wreathed candles and were seen *en masse* in vases, in baskets, in garlands – always as the symbol of divine love.

The rose had become so much a mark of Christian purity that, in 1465, when Pope Pius wanted to send a gift to his home town, Siena, he chose a twenty-seven-inch gold rose, a beautiful object whose dewdrops were meant to convey gratitude. Two bushes were presented by Pius II to Alexander VII and a rose bush was frequently blessed by Pope Gregory the Great, to be sent to sovereigns or churches. Since 1759 the papal Order of the Golden Rose has been reserved for women, mainly Catholic sovereigns. Among the recipients have been Mary Tudor and the Empress Eugénie of France.

At a signal from a nun, little girls often strew petals along the path of a cardinal carrying the Blessed Sacrament, a custom which still exists in Catholic countries. I've seen it in Monaco. How I wish I'd carried a rose to be blessed when Pope John granted me a private audience in 1961.

In ancient Egypt, the rose was sacred to the goddess Isis. The Hebrew Talmud also pays its tribute to the rose: it was written that only rose gardens were to be allowed in Jerusalem, where they have existed since the time of the earliest prophets. When Buddha was preaching once he simply held up a beautiful rose as the sum total of his sermon.

RIGHT: *The Virgin in a Rose Arbour by Stephan Lochner*

In war the rose became symbolic. When Henry VI ruled England in the fifteenth century, law and order broke down. He was king but there were too many private armies with personal and diverse loyalties. The inevitable outcome was civil war. Both sides to the conflict used the rose as a symbol: the Lancastrians, led by the Earls of Suffolk and Somerset, the red; the Yorkists, led by the Earl of Warwick and the tragic Richard Plantagenet, the white.

Even now, the Lancashire Fusiliers Regiment celebrates a landmark victory in its proud history, the battle of Minden in 1759, using their symbol, a red, red rose. On such occasions, champagne is served after dinner in beautiful silver mugs. But if a subaltern is being initiated, a difficult feat has to be performed before he can swallow a drop. He must eat an entire red rose (deposited in the champagne), its short stem and often a leaf as well. It must be chewed carefully and precisely — watched intently by all present, for each has experienced the same tradition. When all has disappeared, the reward is the mugful of

LEFT: *Choosing the red and white roses in the Temple Gardens by Henry Payne*

LEFT: *The Fleur Cowles rose*

champagne, and the young man becomes a member of his mess.

Other wars brought the rose and armies together. Prince Charlie's Scottish Highlanders put the white rose in their bonnets as they marched to England. White roses planted by sympathisers proved their allegiance and signalled that such a house was safe.

The wild rose that grew in Spain wherever conflict took place is called by them *Fior dei Escarmujo*, 'flower of the battle'. In tenth-century Italy, Petrus de Crescentii recommended his followers to close their gardens with hedges of thorny rose bushes and ditches, to secure them against predators.

World War II, despite its horrors, brought a remarkable rose success to life. In 1942, Francis Mielland of France managed to get a few plants of the new rose he had had created to the United States on the last plane from Lyons before the airways were taken over by the Nazis. It was reared by an American nurseryman friend and its official name, Peace, now celebrates the fall of Berlin.

Two French queens were patrons to the greatest rose record of all. Marie Antoinette and the Empress Josephine both helped the deformed painter we know as Pierre-Joseph Redouté. Marie Antoinette summoned him to her court as her Designer in the Cabinet, where he produced the drawings and paintings that have made him the best known botanical painter in art history.

The French Revolution (which sprouted its own terrorism) lost him this royal patronage. Redouté used to visit the deposed Queen in the gloom of her cell in the Temple of Paris before she was guillotined. To cheer her, he brought her roses and his paintings and drawings of flowers.

He was in England when she was actually slain, but returned to his second royal patron, the Empress Josephine Bonaparte, who retained him after peace was restored to France. She, too, was in love with roses, and together she and Redouté reshaped a deserted garden in the château named Malmaison (in Revil, not far down the

Marie Antoinette by L C Clay. The tragic queen who loved roses and was patron to Pierre-Joseph Redouté

River Seine from Paris), which she bought, transformed and made famous while Napoleon was conquering Egypt in 1799. Roses were allotted an enormous area, making Malmaison the most memorable rose garden ever seen. During the early days, Napoleon's love for her was strong enough for him to take along a botanist when fighting wars, his job to send back roses from the battlefields. After Napoleon was crowned Emperor he lost interest in Josephine; she divorced him in 1809 but continued to use Malmaison. She died in May 1814, aged fifty, of a cold caught at a reception for Tsar Alexander I.

The garden must have given solace to the unhappy lonely woman who was obviously trying to recreate her past as a light-hearted little girl in Martinique, the tropical, paradisical island where she was born; the former Marie Joséphine Rose Tascher de la Pagerie became Napoleon's bride.

She bought more than two hundred and fifty rose varieties from four continents, with extravagant disregard for price. Despite the turbulence of the Napoleonic Wars, dispensation was arranged for an English gardener, John Kennedy, to bring her roses, passing safely from England's coast to France. Pierre Redouté assisted her in garden design and in

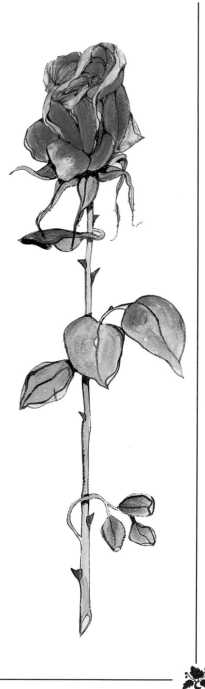

Roses were an integral part of the décor in the palace of Versailles as shown in this photograph of Marie Antoinette's bedroom

keeping botanical records, and examples of those illustrations still exist. Many were merely painted as botanical book-keeping but how they enrich our eyes today! Ironically, Josephine never saw them reproduced; she was already dead when the first set of plates was published in 1817.

Meticulous, sensitive and beautiful, Redouté's prints and paintings are collectors' items today, and vast prices are recorded in auction rooms for them. One book recently sold for almost £60,000. On his deathbed, one of his poorest students brought him a single flower, and Redouté, the recorder of at least a thousand botanical species, suffered his final stroke while holding not a rose but this lily in his hand.

The Frontispiece from 'Les Rosier' by Pierre-Joseph Redouté

I n art, the rose, in itself a work of art, had an extraordinary place; no flower has ever served the painter better. The early treatments were interpretations of religious and mythical ideas, but slowly these evolved to become the realistic subjects which touched viewers' hearts.

The earliest painted rose I have seen is the one on the walls of Knossos at Crete, and China's ancient flower paintings go back to the tenth century. In sixteenth-century Holland, flowers were cheaper to have painted than they were to buy and thus began the rush of commissions by the rich to record their ownership of this important status symbol. Hence the marriage of art and botany. Even nurserymen employed masters to illustrate their catalogues.

I am always fascinated by the bugs, bees, predatory snails and even snakes which the artists added as signs of versatility; all were laden with allegorical images, superstitions and fables. The caterpillar was for man, the butterfly for his soul, lizards, frogs and snakes for death. Birds, shells, other insects and fruit also climbed into many of the same crowded canvasses.

The French perfected printing techniques so

Spring by Arcimboldo. An example of 16th-century floral painting taken to the extreme where the picture is made of flowers

flawlessly that prints originally commissioned as botanical records — mainly for kings, bishops and the fashionable rich — also became works of art. One very beautiful example is Nicholas Robert's gaily red and white striped 'Rosa Mundi', drawn in 1640. Thousands of faithful drawings were produced, and fine examples can now be seen at the *Institut des Plantes* in Paris.

In Holland, Jan Brueghel's creative forces were torrential. He packed canvasses with enough flowers to leave one breathless — and produced them fast (while Van Aelst took four days just to paint one carnation). They assembled so many flowers in one painting it made a nonsense of the seasons. Spring, summer, autumn and winter flowers mingle together as if they grew simultaneously. One can almost smell the fragrance of these roses.

Self-portrait of the artist with roses by Marc Chagall

Many, many other names come to mind (not all — and not in any historic order): Johann Laurents Jensen, Van den Bosch, Graham Sutherland, Verelst, Mary Moser, Odilon Redon, Gaudi, Fantin-Latour, Fragonard, Cezanne, Manet, Menoyer, Jan de Heem, Jan van Huysum, Balthazar, Delacroix, Bonnard, Kyss, even Chagall had a religious regard for flowers.

In three hundred years, although they are assumed to have done at least half of the paintings, few women achieved permanent places in art. In these corsetted centuries, Mary Lawrance's *A Collection of*

Roses in a Cup by Fantin-Latour. A fine example from a master painter of these beautiful flowers

The Birth of Venus by Botticelli. The goddess of love rises from the sea in a shower of roses

Roses from Nature, published between 1796 and 1799, was the first to be devoted exclusively to the rose, with text and hand-coloured engravings of her own works.

I always think of Botticelli: who else would paint roses as spray coming from the sea – as he did in his *Birth of Venus?*

Pressing flowers has made an artist of many non-painters. The first was recorded in 1545 when a teacher of medicine pressed a flower so as to be able to study it. The late Princess Grace of Monaco pressed flowers in her free time and made a most successful Paris exhibition.

The Naif painter Le Douanier Rousseau immortalised the Victorian love of the rose in one small delicious painting, modestly, as a French birthday card. I saw it in Charles Laughton's collection in Hollywood and have never forgotten it.

Albrecht Dürer established his reputation with the *Madonna of the Roses* which he painted in Venice early in the sixteenth century, and when I see his magical little drawing of a bunch of violets, I wish he'd done one of roses on their own. And I often wonder if the late Georgia O'Keeffe, who painted such vivid poppies and other flowers, had lived in rose country and not the desert, how she would have painted the living rose?

Renoir's ancestors in Utrecht loved moss roses and

two centuries later so did Renoir himself. But many roses painted today are pretentious; others magical – those of the gifted Chilean painter Claudio Bravo are extraordinary. His exquisite rose is worthy of comparison to any of the masters. Yes, even Dürer.

Although he rarely painted them, Georges Braque always had flowers to hand in his studios in Paris and Varengeville near Dieppe which I often visited before he died. Flowers cut in the garden were just placed in the handiest containers. I've seen jugs, crocks and kitchen glasses. None were consciously 'done-up' for an effect. Never. They were there because Braque had to be surrounded by flowers; his wife kept them before him in a most casual, non-intrusive way. I found this a heart-warming testament of this man's love and need for flowers.

A rose by Claudio Bravo.
An exquisite example of this
much-painted flower

LEFT: *Roman de la Rose. The lover attains the Rose and the love of his sweetheart?*

I n literature, we have only to read Shakespeare. Omar Khayyám asked: 'Why dost thou sell the rose for silver? For what more precious than the rose can money buy?' Confucius says that the Imperial Chinese had six hundred books on roses in 500 BC. Goethe described the rose as nature's supreme creation. In the *Iliad*, Homer is eloquent about Achilles' shield of roses. Pliny listed the twelve Roman roses he loved.

Gertrude Stein, in her book *Sacred Emily* (studded with symbolism), took eight words to immortalise her affection: 'A rose is a rose is a rose', a phrase she had written around the edge of a plate – her personal gesture to the infinity of the flower which became her crest. Chaucer had his Apothecaries' Rose from Provins near Paris, the star of his *Roman de la Rose* and said also to be the red rose of Lancaster.

By the time of the troubadour, in Richard the Lionheart's day, poetry owed much to the rose. Nightingales and roses were entwined in glittering little songs.

But although the roses reminded every proud knight of the Blessed Virgin, and also made him think of his lady love, it was not together. Sacred and profane love, he knew must never, never intermingle.

Dante, in his *Divine Comedy*, written early in the fourteenth century, describes Beatrice as drawing him into Paradise which, legend has it, was itself designed as a rose.

There are other examples among many thousands. In the Bible one reads, 'The desert shall rejoice and blossom as the rose,' while Solomon advised his followers, 'Let us crown ourselves with rosebuds.' And among the sixty or more rose-references in his works, Shakespeare's probably best remembered is his 'What's in a name? That which we call a rose by any other name would smell as sweet.' Edward Lear, in a jocular mood, wrote: 'R was once a little rose, Rosy, Posy, Mosy.'

D.H. Lawrence wrote many poems about roses and opened the collection he called *Nettles* with a provocative poem about the flower. Thomas Moore gave us 'Tis the last

LEFT: *A young man wearing a rose-painted cloak against a rose tree by Nicholas Hilliard*

Rose of Summer.' Robert Burns, in his 'O my love is like a red, red rose,' made it an enduring love token. Neither Keats, Robert Browning, Thackeray nor Tennyson ignored the rose in their work. Tennyson wrote: 'Saints are virgins; they love the white rose of virginity.'

Once I gave a dinner for Karen Blixen, the author of *Seven Gothic Tales* and *Out of Africa*, not long before she died. She arrived wearing a brown chiffon shirt dress with a tiny train. Neckline and wrists were ruffled and in a black velvet belt around her tiny waist she had tucked one ravishing rose. Everyone was reminded of Camille.

Even Oscar Wilde wrote a fable coupling the rose with a nightingale which died a martyr for the student who longed for a rose to give the maiden with whom he was passionately in love. And didn't Alice in Wonderland find it a curious thing for three gardeners to be painting white roses red to please a queen?

Mythology also cosseted the rose, leaving more fables about this blossom than about any other flower. Whenever I look at my moss roses, I am reminded of the myth (attributed to the Germans) about moss on the ground: its low tiny growth, which has no scent or flower, was so pleasant to the touch that when Christ entered one such green glade, he cooled his feet on the soft springiness. As he passed, the first moss *rose* sprang up! This rose, also thought to be the blood of Christ, drop by drop on mossy soil at the foot of the Cross, is back in our gardens after years of abandonment.

One American tale concerns the dark red Grant rose. In an Indian uprising in Florida in 1835, a farmer called Grant was attacked by marauding Indians, and mutilated and killed in the forest. They then turned back to plunder his home, catching up with his wife and child as they fled, hacking them to death – soaking the ground in blood. A beautiful dark red rose grows on the spot today, a memorial to the Grant family tragedy.

Other legends abound in different cultures. Aphrodite anointed the dead Hector with rose perfume. Diana turned her current fickle paramour

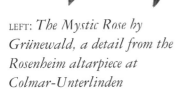

LEFT: *The Mystic Rose by Grünewald, a detail from the Rosenheim altarpiece at Colmar-Unterlinden*

into a rose, past lovers into its thorns. The Turkish say the rose was born from the sweat of Mohammed. Another is about Eve; she was supposed to have created the red rose when she bent to kiss a bud. As she did, the pale flower blushed deep red.

The Rose of the Flower Martyrs is another grim tale of the past: a beautiful maiden had been tied to a stake to be punished for a crime she did not commit. When the fire was lit, it immediately went out. All the scorched faggots turned into red roses and the unkindled ones became white ones, the episode making the rose a mystical object for all who gathered there.

So in love were Tristan and Isolde that their two graves produced intertwining roses. Jousting knights wore a rose embroidered on their sleeves, for beauty was the reward for bravery. There is

Drawing of a design for a bathroom ceiling by Robert Adam

*The Heart of the Rose by
Burne-Jones. Or should it be
the heart is in the rose?*

more: the rose is offered in houses of piety; and sent
to assuage grief. It was offered against witchcraft
and led prisoners to the scaffold. What other flower
has such versatility?

The village girl chosen as the most virtuous in
France still wears a crown of roses, its thorns
protecting her virginity. The complexion of a
beautiful English girl is described as 'like a rose'.

Prayer-beads (the Rosary) which slip through millions of fingers are often made of the hardened paste of hips, for some of the first rosaries were simply rose-hips strung together.

If one is in pain, it is '*no* bed of roses'; if life is good, one's 'path is strewn with roses' or you see life 'through rose-coloured spectacles'. In mediaeval times, when a rose was suspended from a ceiling, its message was clear to men below that all conversation must be confidential – hence the much misused term of our time: *sub-rosa*. Later in the sixteenth century Pope Hadrian VI decreed that a rose must be carved on the confessional so for Roman Catholics the rose became a sign of confidentiality. Today, we find a rose carved in the central plasterwork on the ceiling of the finest Georgian drawing rooms.

In the language of flowers a spray of many white rosebuds signifies secrecy, the yellow rose infidelity or jealousy. The yellow rose is also the State of Texas's flower; but can a Texan be jealous of *anything*?

The rose is of course England's national flower and

it is also the emblem of Czechoslovakia, Honduras, Poland, Romania and Iran. In the US it has been adopted by the states of Georgia, of New York, Iowa and North Dakota.

'Talking to the rose' is not new. Zen Buddhists started the practice many centuries ago; westerners translate it into today's superb flower care. Some may think this is mad or just plain eccentric. I don't. By the way, the term 'to be a secondhand rose' probably came from Henry II's mistress, Rosamond Clifford, who was installed by him in a house inside a maze. This secondhand woman died young, poisoned, some said, by Henry's jealous and powerful wife, Eleanor of Aquitaine.

A Jewish legend equates the pink rose with Paradise, where a man went to beautify his tent with dozens of roses. At dusk the reflection of the fiery sun setting on the rose seemed to represent Hell in flame.

Music, too, has been captivated by the rose. In opera, there is shining evidence of the rose's diverse nature: Richard Strauss's *Der Rosenkavalier* is based on the bygone German custom by which a cavalier presented a silver rose to his love. One of Sir Arthur Sullivan's comic operas is called *The Rose of Persia*. Leo Fall composed *The Rose of Istanbul*. In *Merrie England* Sir Walter Raleigh is in love with a lady-in-waiting to Queen Elizabeth I, whom he calls 'The Rose of England'. In Friedrich von Flotow's *Martha* she sings to her employer about the last rose of summer – little knowing that he is really the Earl of Derby. Nor does he realise that she is, in reality, Maid of Honour to Queen Anne. Of such situations are operas made.

A much-beloved example is in an 'everyday' song. Nat King Cole's voice will probably never die on records and cassettes; his dulcet serenade to 'The Rambling Rose' should live forever. 'Roses of Picardy' is another song which already shows a touch of posterity.

Nijinsky's name has a magical place in ballet – and rose-history. His legendary *Le Spectre de la Rose*, that most poetic ballet first seen in 1911,

LEFT: *Le Spectre de la Rose.*
The great Nijinsky in
costume in 1911

was based on Théophile Gautier's poem, translated into ballet by Fokine for Diaghilev's Ballets Russes. Nijinsky danced dressed as a rose, in a costume and set designed by Léon Bakst. Together, all four creators produced a dream world on stage. It should be recreated. We remember, too, Margot Fonteyn's 'Rose Adagio' ballet.

LEFT: *The Mogul Emperor in his Persian garden*

The importance of scent-power in a rose garden cannot be over-estimated since the sense of smell is ten thousand times more sensitive than that of taste. Narcissi, daphne, mock orange (Philadelphus), lilac and others make their own fragrant statements but so do such lovely roses as the cabbage rose, the *Rosa Alba*, Papa Meilland, Josephine Bruce, the moss rose and such climbers as Albertine and Caroline Testou – and, if procurable, the *Rosa Noisettiana* or Blush Noisette which was once a favourite at Josephine's Malmaison. Nature must have been absolutely incensed when roses were robbed of their scent. Katharine White, of the superb botanic essays, once wrote that 'a rose without a smell is only half a rose'.

Scent practically vanished at one time but the tide has turned. Older roses (as well as new inventions) are finding their way into our gardens again through fragrance, now one of their most qualifying ingredients. The old damask rose is back with its clove-like perfume, as in ancient times – so strong it can scent the air. If we could have smelled some of the earliest roses, their fragrance would probably have made us think of many fruits. Try to guess whether the rose you now grow can be compared to an apricot, a pear, a melon, to aubergines or the crushed leaves of green tea plant, or to such animal substances as musk or honey.

For millennia the rose was treasured for the way its perfume survived when the petals were dried.

Then came the distillation of rose-water, a substance that in ancient and mediaeval times was believed to cure many ills. The much more precious otto or attar of roses, an oil that floats on the surface of rose-water, was worth more than its weight in gold. It is said to have been discovered at the court of the Moghul Emperor Djihangur when the Persian Princess Nour-Djihan gave a splendid party for her husband. There are two versions of the story: that the Princess's mother noticed a strongly perfumed foam forming on the rivulets of rose-water that ran through the garden, and that the Princess herself skimmed off the oil with her handkerchief while being rowed across the lake.

Nowadays attar is produced mainly in Bulgaria and Turkish Anatolia, from damask and gallic roses. In France it is usually extracted from cabbage roses using a solvent. Once, when I was an official guest of Grasse in France, I watched mountainous piles of petals being mixed with a measured quantity before being put into an *alambic* to be pulped. The sweet smell was sweated out drop by drop by drop and in the process seemed to perfume a whole city. How does one define the scent of rose perfume? Once I heard a young Japanese woman describe it to Princess Grace of Monaco as a 'high society' smell. I wondered how that young woman chose her own scent. Did she use it as a reflection of her personality, her life-style or, most important of all, her taste? The choice says something of any woman who uses perfume.

RIGHT: *17th-century embroidered cushion cover with silk and metal threads*

LEFT: *16th-century Portrait of a Lady. A fine example of English embroidery*

The rose is also immortalised within the house. Since the sixteenth century, needlewomen have turned to it for ideas; roses became their favourite design – for weavers as well. Both copied Dutch naturalistic paintings.

Today, men as well as women embroider roses on firescreens, bellpulls, footstools, kneelers, tea caddies, pictures and picture frames, decorated blankets and patchwork. (Both the Duke of Windsor

and his brother George VI were constant needlepointers.) Antique needlepoint carpets of roses are costly heirlooms today as are Persian and Bokhara carpets that so often display the rose. In lace when the rose is used as a focal point it is called rose-point. And now yuppies wear expensive knitted sweaters and dresses which have become gardens of roses. 'Trellis', the first wallpaper William Morris designed, depicts a red climbing rose said to be taken from one at his home in Bexley Heath; and Augustus Pugin created a delightfully modern-looking 'Rose and Coronet' paper for the Houses of Parliament.

What would that most English of fabrics, chintz, be without the rose? It appeared first in the sixteenth and early seventeenth centuries imported from India, its name derived from the Sanskrit word for 'variegated'. Produced later in England also, by 1700 parliament had to legislate – and again in 1721 – against both importing and manufacturing these printed fabrics since they were

Sèvres porcelain vase, French 18th century

doing so much harm to the local producers of linen, wool and silk.

Jacobite glasses were etched with roses. Opaque white glass for toasts to the king 'over the water' and featuring the rose was made in Bristol as late as the 1880s. In Clichy and Baccarat paperweights the rose is almost a signature. The rose also invaded the world of porcelain, especially in Sèvres and Meissen. Madame de Pompadour used to surround herself with banks of porcelain roses when she was receiving her royal lover, Louis XV. In her bedroom, now restored at Versailles, roses dance on canopy, curtains, upholstery – and always on her lavishly rose-embroidered gowns. The ubiquitous fresh rose was always tucked in her bosom and, jewelled, in her hair.

In all *objets d'art*, the rose was and is an inspiration. A most enduring and unmatched art was born in the workshop of the man who was recognised and commissioned by Czar Nicholas II. He was the genius called Carl Fabergé, whose name is also hallowed by today's collectors.

The only piece by Carl Fabergé to feature a rose alone

The SICK ROSE

O Rose, thou art sick.
The invisible worm.
That flies in the night
In the howling storm:

Has found out thy bed
Of crimson joy:
And his dark secret love
Does thy life destroy.

LEFT: *The Sick Rose from Songs of Innocence by William Blake*

S ince time immemorial, the rose has been a source of medicine, the illuminated manuscripts of Dioscorides being one of the oldest records of medical flower-lore in existence, while the Roman Pliny mentions thirty-two remedies that roses supplied.

Not too many decades ago, throughout Europe, roses were chiefly grown to strew about houses – particularly in times of plague. The petals (*en masse*) were expected to counteract the lack of sanitation and to help eliminate smells, including those of the illnesses of the time. King Edward I's 1306 Bill of Medicines made special reference to *Rosa gallica*, which he believed had been brought to Europe from the 'Land of the Saracens'. The seventeenth-century English herbalist Nicholas Culpeper particularly valued this 'Apothecaries' Rose' for treatment of disorders in the head, eyes, gums and stomach, and in Victorian times it was grown extensively in Surrey for the use of London druggists.

Today, some modern medical science has gone forward by looking backwards, re-thinking ancient flower remedies so that some are the subject of respectable research today. It is no longer debated

that enormous amounts of vitamin C can be
extracted from the plushy flesh of the rose-hip.
Herbalists, in fact, claim there is more of this vital
vitamin, measure for measure, in rose-hips than in
oranges. Among the famous flower remedies
devised by Dr Edward Bach, extract of Wild Rose is
the specific for apathy and resignation. Probably the
most valued spokesman of herbal medicine today is
the Prince of Wales, who calmly continues to
discuss the controversial subject of holistic
treatment and to give many forms of alternative
therapy his support.

One of Elizabeth I's counsellors, Francis Bacon, wrote about gardens: 'Only God Almighty could have planted one ... God was good.' Every rose garden reinforces that idea.

Gardens are places which allow us to surround ourselves with an area *we* create; they show us up for what we are – can even reveal our character. Are we generous or miserly, warm or cool? Do we have a friendly garden or a tight ungiving one? To be beautiful, regardless of size, a rose garden needs love – which Beverly Nichols, the famed author-gardener, once told me was his first essential. He could always tell whether or not a garden had received its proper share.

Tending a garden has been done in many ways, some of them eccentric. The rose authority Francis B Lester gave advice in his book published in 1942, *My Friend the Rose*. He claimed that a big beef bone (cooked or raw – either would do) should be buried under rose bushes, 'to allow the roots to climb down to embrace and feed on the decaying object in the darkness below'. Like most gardeners, however, I let my bushes thrive on aged manure and good soil.

There is one canard I'd love to destroy; that rose gardens hate big cities, surviving only in air which must be a clean and smokeless atmosphere. Throughout the horrors of bombing, fire and the smoke-laden air in and around London and other big cities during the last war, whatever cherished space was available to grow the much-needed survival food always included at least one cherished rose. In that world of crowded streets, the smallest garden had a rose standing tall amidst the food. This habit continues; today roses bloom in the same cramped terraces in England's Midlands and North in great good health. Bricklayers, mechanics, labourers, men and women, all show their devotion – there are no divisions.

Having two very different gardens, one in England's green Sussex and the other in dry Spain, I have to deal with two different challenges. In England, there are the expected separate garden areas – with lakes and water gardens, the long herbaceous border, separate rose gardens and an orchard. Each requires a different solution; for example I plant only white roses, white lilacs, white geraniums, white tulips and white tobacco plants against the dark back walls of our ancient barn.

In Spain's Extremadura the land is so barren

PREVIOUS PAGE: *The Lady in the Garden by Claude Monet (detail). The master Impressionist did not only paint waterlilies*

and ungiving, the sixteenth-century Conquistadors were easily recruited there, glad to leave to go to America; but I have managed to create a green, green Moorish garden (including the sound of rippling water the Moors loved so well) around my ancient castle. I planted green palms, figs, olive and cypress trees. Pinky-beige stone has its own decor with tall, very tall agapanthus that look like statuesque sentinels parading below the walls. Pale blue plumbago entwines with fragrant white jasmine. In a separate area I massed together one hundred of my own pale Fleur Cowles roses.

How was this possible in such arid land? The miracle owes itself to the cistern (large as a pond!) which lies under the castle itself. Whenever I look outside my walls at the dry land surrounding my restored national monument I thank those Moorish conquerors. It is only their supply of extra water underground, topped up every time it rains, that makes my garden such an unexpected surprise.

The Arabs loved their rose gardens, for to them they symbolised a sensual perception of Islamic Paradise, the image which is in the words and works of their philosophers and poets. The gardens in Spain's Alhambra reflect The Moors' love of roses which I believe they inherited from the Persians after their invasion of Persia in the seventh century.

LEFT: *William Morris used flowers in many of his designs. This example is the Trellis Design, one of this best and of course it features roses*

To visit rose gardens is the aim of all good
travellers, but I'm grateful to the gods that I
was able, thirty-odd years ago (long before it
became difficult), to get to Kashmir. It was a
paradise for rose lovers especially the route from
the airport to the city of Srinagar. The road was
bordered by a massive fringe of tiny five-
petalled roses pushing their way through the
stones *en route*. Bushes, many of them roses,
crowded the meadows alongside.

The beautiful Dal Lake, once the centrepiece
of Kashmir, has now become a casualty, reduced
in size from its former fourteen square miles to
the current seven. Tourist houseboats have been
emptying raw garbage into it, and viral
hepatitis is one curse that follows. 'Floating
gardens' and weeds choke it; trees disappear.
Birds – the skylarks, grey heron, fishing eagles,
the pheasant-tailed jacana – sing no more.

Because I have that home in the heart of
Spain, I must of necessity drive through Madrid
to get there. Madrid's rose garden, the Roselede
del Parque del Oeste, is worth anyone's detour.
Some call it the most beautiful rose garden in
the world. It was planted in 1954 on what was
once a rubbish dump on the steep slope not far
below the Royal Palace and there is a fine view
from the Paseo de Rosales above.

In Rome, the Roseto di Roma was planted in 1928 on the ruins of Nero's palace. It is now a vast amphitheatre of over a thousand old and new varieties. In Baden-Baden, the rose garden is one visitors don't miss.

In the United States (although I haven't lived there for many years), I do know (and remember and visit) many splendid rose gardens. The oldest, often called the best, is in Portland, Oregon; another is the Hershey Rose Garden in Pennsylvania which houses three museums as well as twenty-three acres of roses. At the Nature Centre of Mystic, Connecticut, descriptions of each rose are written in Braille for the pleasure of those who cannot see (but, hopefully, can smell).

The USA can boast some incredible statistics. The Samuell-Grand Municipal Garden in Dallas is, in outsize Texan terms, America's largest commercial rose garden. There one finds pools, fountains, sunken garden terraces and gazebos — enhanced by thirty thousand roses.

At Tampa, Florida the rose gardens of the Doge's Palace in Venice have been recreated by the Ringling Brothers of circus fame. An equally spectacular rose garden is maintained at the late William Randolph Hearst's San Simeon castle in California, where the former newspaper magnet and Marion Davies once lived.

In the first American municipal garden in Elizabeth Park, West Hartford, Connecticut fifteen thousand roses offer quantities of ideas.

A public rose garden in Monaco, a memorial to Princess Grace, was created by Prince Rainier just after her death, on land he reclaimed from the sea. The principal rose growers of Europe gave beautiful superbly identified rose bushes. The result is a pleasure to all who visit it.

In the Princess's own garden in the Palace the rose named for her and the one named for me live together. Having a rose with your name is a modest and I think privileged form of immortality, a pleasure shared with countless others, including royalty and many botanical experts.

A tour of France brings exciting pleasure, beginning (after Malmaison, of course) with Paris's L'Hay-les-Roses with its rose arches and pergolas inspired by Empress Josephine's gardens. To the French, it represents the ideal. L'Hay is bounded by walks covered in roses, many climbing over trellises, with generous quantities of weeping standards in each but nothing helter-skelter. Go in June before tourists pile in; roses are at their loveliest then.

One of L'Hay's many lavish owners, before it

RIGHT: *The Gardens of L'Hay-les-Roses in the suburbs of Paris*

became the property of the city of Paris, was the proprietor of the Paris department store called Bon Marché, Jules Gravereaux, who vied with Josephine's Malmaison in the astronomic size of his collection. By 1900, aided by the landscape artist Edouard André, he had gathered together three thousand varieties of roses, filling L'Hay with stunning effect. In the centre of the garden he built a library of roses, paintings, drawings, books, pottery, stamps and textiles in an unmatched collection. Sadly, it was stolen in 1980 and undoubtedly sold piece by piece. The rose garden was spared.

The gardens at the Château de Bagatelle in the Bois de Boulogne were designed in 1905 by Jean-Claude Forestier, then Paris's Conservateur des Jardins. He was a friend of Monet and an admirer of the Impressionist school of painting and this is reflected in the striking use of colour and daring juxtapositions that characterise the displays of roses there. At Monet's own garden, now restored at Giverny, north of Paris, a weeping rose is curved over a bamboo arch in a wonderful romantic display.

There are many other gardens in Paris to visit – the one at rue des Abondance, for instance, called the Jardin Albert Kahn for the man who laid it out in the early 1900s; it is now owned by

RIGHT: *Male and female roses, painted by Graham Sutherland for the author*

the city. Though small compared to Bagatelle and L'Hay, it has a heart-warming beauty – but less stylised, for the lover of informal gardens.

Sir Richard Wallace, who gave the Wallace Collection of great paintings to the British nation, built water troughs all over Paris for thirsty horses in the horse-and-buggy era. I found many of these troughs in Maurice Chevalier's garden on the city outskirts when I went to lunch with him. He'd bought all he could as they fell out of use to decorate his highly personal garden and as containers for his roses.

Turkey's Topkapi Palace in Istanbul is the fabled mecca for one of the world's most blazing collections of royal jewels, but the gems are outshone in the rose garden outside, where fifty thousand only white roses grow. Such extravagance reflects that of a sixteenth-century sultan. He had another rose garden so enormous it took men on horseback five days to ride through the flowers planted to provide for his outrageous demands.

In England roses are part of the culture and there are many public rose gardens. I recommend one at my back door, at Wisley in Surrey, the home of the Royal Horticultural Society. The Garden Walk at Chartwell, also in

Surrey, the family home of Sir Winston and Lady Churchill, was planted in1958 by the Churchill family in celebration of their parents' golden anniversary. In London, despite the traffic, I find it worthwhile to detour to Queen Mary's rose garden in full bloom in Regent's Park; conceived and named for her in 1930, it is a feast for the eye.

Other examples of inspired rose gardens can be found at the Royal National Rose Society near St Albans not far from London, where thirty thousand roses flourish in twelve acres at Bone Hill in Hertfordshire. It is a must and especially at the time of the Rose Festival in early June. There are other places to visit on day trips from London: Charleston Manor in West Dean, West Sussex; the noted Astor estate, now a hotel near Maidenhead in Berkshire; Sissinghurst Castle in Kent (which simply must not be missed). For me, the best there is its beautiful all-white garden created by Vita Sackville-West.

Many plants such as the rose of Jericho, the Christian rose, rose of Sharon, Lenten and Christmas rose, rock or sun rose, tuberose, Cherokee rose, rose geranium, primrose, rosemary, rose acacia and rose campion call themselves roses but this should fool no one. They are not roses at all – it is just *floral envy.*

But the true rose can and does grow everywhere on earth; it crosses geographic boundaries which otherwise separate nations, and keeps the best and the worst possible company, moving from king to peon, from gardens which are the hobby and love of the rich to the tin cans of the poor, hanging on walls and by the doorways of peasants in so many corners of the world. I love to see the tough old stems of aged bushes holding up the roses alongside ramshackle homes in remote Spanish villages. To me, these simple sights are the greatest compliment to the rose.

The Mexicans, among others, have built roses into their culture. There is a lovely legend, based upon a story of roses, that is celebrated in a painting of a humble man, which hangs in the nearly ruined chapel connected to the Guadalupe

LEFT: *Our Lady of Cocracas, Cuzco, Peru*

Cathedral in Mexico City. The story is touching: this peasant had walked high into the mountains where he had seen a vision of the Virgin, then was accosted by men who demanded that he disclose whatever he was hiding. He insisted he had nothing – but when his apron was opened and spread out, it was full of beautiful roses! No roses grew anywhere in those stark hills.

Other rose myths in Mexico concern life and death. Death? Yes, sadly, for to them a child must have roses strewn over its grave. Life? Yes, in the happy proverb that says: 'When a man wears a rose in his hat, he owns the whole world.'

I quite understand this. Once upon a time, I rented a house for a vacation in Cuernavacca, Mexico. Its memory is indelible; there was a garden, which I can still see in my mind's eye, heavy with perfect roses. One sunset, I bent over to pluck the pinkest, largest, most fragrant rose I had ever seen (the size of a small cabbage) until I realised that hidden inside its curled petals, terrifyingly, sat a spider – a tarantula! Later, still shaking, that horrid experience was erased from my mind when the same rose, now *uninhabited*, was presented to me by the gardener. Looking at its incredible beauty, I suddenly felt like that man with a rose in his hat.

The rose has no sexual bias: men as well as women love it, buy it, grow it, give it. But the rose itself is always a 'she'. However, if you transpose the letters of its name it becomes Eros, god of love.

ACKNOWLEDGMENTS

The publishers wish to thank all those listed below for permission to reproduce illustrations in this book (unless otherwise indicated original paintings are by the author):

Cover illustration – *The Baccarat Rose* Fleur Cowles

Pages i, iii, 74 – *The Baccarat Rose* Fleur Cowles

Page vi – *Tree of Life, India 18thC* Visual Arts Library/Detroit Institute of Art

Page 1 – *Reverse of Drachma coin, Rhodes 4thC BC* Peter Clayton

Pages 2 (detail), 44/5, 71 (detail) – *Trilogy* Fleur Cowles

Page 3 – *Top of the Grand Staircase, Knossos* Peter Clayton

Page 4 – *An Allegory with Venus and Cupid by Bronzino* The National Gallery, London

Page 6 – *Desert Rose* Fleur Cowles

Pages 7 (detail), 15, 60/1 (detail), 67 (detail) – *Flying Roses* Fleur Cowles

Page 8 – *Coronation of the Virgin by Velázquez* Museo del Prado, Madrid

Page 9 – *South Rose window, Angers Cathedral c1463* Bridgeman Art Library

Pages 10 and 52 (detail) – *Golden World* Fleur Cowles

Page 11 – *The Virgin in a Rose Arbour by Stephan Lochner* Bridgeman Art Library/Wallraf-Richartz Museum, Cologne

Page 12 – *Choosing the red and white roses in the Temple Gardens by Henry Payne* Bridgeman Art Library/Courtesy of Birmingham City Museums & Art Gallery

Page 13 – *Rose Cover* Fleur Cowles

Page 14 – *The Fleur Cowles rose* Fleur Cowles

Page 16 – *Marie Antoinette by L C Clay* Guildhall Art Gallery, London

Page 17 – *Circular Scarf* Fleur Cowles

Pages 18 (detail), 41 – *Untitled* Fleur Cowles

Page 19 (top) – *Marie Antoinette's bedroom, Palace of Versailles, France 18thC* Visual Arts Library

Page 19 (bottom) – *Frontispiece for 'Les Rosier' by Pierre-Joseph Redouté 1817* Bridgeman Art Library/Linnean Society, London

Page 20 – *Tupperware Rose* Fleur Cowles

Page 21 – *Spring by Arcimboldo 16thC* Visual Arts Library/ The Louvre, Paris

Page 22 – *Self-portrait by Marc Chagall 1914* Visual Arts Library/Private Collection

Page 23 – *Roses in a Cup by Fantin-Latour 1882* Visual Arts Library/Musée d'Orsay, Paris

Pages 24 and 25 (detail) – *The Birth of Venus by Sandro Botticelli 1440-1510* Bridgeman Art Library/Galleria degli Uffizi, Florence

Page 26 – *Diptych* Fleur Cowles

Pages 27 and 69 (detail) – *Rose by Claudio Bravo* Fleur Cowles

Page 28 – *Roman de la Rose: Lover attains the Rose Harley MS 4425, folio 184b, Flemish c1500* Bridgeman Art Library/ British Museum

Page 29 (detail) – *Limbo* Fleur Cowles

Page 30 – *Miniature of a young man against a rose tree by Nicholas Hilliard 1547-1619* Bridgeman Art Library/ Courtesy of the Trustees of the Victoria and Albert Museum, London

Page 31 – *Trio* Fleur Cowles

Page 32 (detail) – *The Mystic Rose, Rosenheim alterpiece, Colmar-Unterlinden by Grünewald 1505-16* Visual Arts Library

Page 33 – *The Rose* Fleur Cowles